SECRET HISTORY

THE WAR ON TERROR

SECRET HISTORY

THE WAR ON TERROR

BRIAN WILLIAMS

ARCTURUS

Reprinted in 2012
This edition first published in 2010 by Arcturus Publishing
Distributed by Black Rabbit Books
P.O. Box 3263
Mankato
Minnesota MN 56002

Printed in The United States of America

Series concept: Alex Woolf
Editors: Karen Taschek and Alex Woolf
Designer: Tall Tree
Picture researcher: Alex Woolf

Library of Congress Cataloging-in-Publication Data

Williams, Brian, 1943-
    The war on terror / Brian Williams.
        p. cm. – (Secret history)
    Includes index.
    Summary: "This high-interest series, aimed at reluctant
readers, looks at secret campaigns behind the major
conflicts of the past 100 years. Biographical sidebars
focus on heroic or notorious personalities. Highlighted
fact features include special operations and their results,
resistance movements, propaganda and the history of
the time - as is known....and not readily known"–
Provided by publisher.
    ISBN 978-1-84837-699-1 (library binding)
    1. Terrorism–Prevention–United States–Juvenile
literature. 2. War on Terrorism, 2001-2009–Juvenile
literature. 3. September 11 Terrorist Attacks, 2001–
Juvenile literature. I. Title.
    HV6432.W545 2011
    973.931–dc22

                        2010011013

SL000973US
Supplier 02, Date 1012, Print Run 2306

Picture credits:
Corbis: 6 (Sean Adair/Reuters), 7 (Reuters), 9 (Jim
Hollander Files/epa), 10 (Federico Gambarini/epa),
11 (Matt Dunham/Reuters), 13 (Raminder Pal Singh/
epa), 14 (Francis R Malasig/epa), 15 (The Stocktrek
Corp/Brand X), 16 (Ron Sachs/CNP), 19 (al-Jazeera
Television/Reuters), 20 (George Steinmetz), 21 (Thierry
Prat/Sygma), 22 (Mike Stewart/Sygma), 23 (Ramin
Talaie), 25 (Ron Sachs/CNP/Sygma), 27 (Carl
Schulze/dpa), 29 (John Hayes/Reuters), 32 (Rahat
Dar/epa), 33 (Reuters), 35 (Reuters), 36 (Reuters), 37
(Reuters), 39 (Phillip Dhil/epa), 42 (S Sabawoon/epa),
43 (Amr Abdallah Dalsh/Reuters).
Getty Images: cover *right* and 8 (AFP), 17 (Pavel
Horejs), 18 (CNN), 28 (Abid Katib), 30, 31 (David
Silverman), 34 (Scott Nelson), 38 (Abikar/AFP), 40
(Massoud Hossaini/AFP), 41 (Mauricio Lima/AFP).
Science Photo Library: 26 (NASA/DFRC).
Shutterstock: cover *bottom left* (terekhov igor), 12 (Perov
Stanislav), 24 (edobric).

Cover illustrations: *top left*: A postcard of New York
City showing the Twin Towers; *bottom left*: A laptop
computer; *right*: Osama bin Laden.

Spread heading illustrations are all from Shutterstock: 6:
airliner (T-Design); 8, 34, 38: submachine gun (Maxim
Urievich Lysenko); 10, 14, 18: cell phone (Sergey
Peterman); 12, 20, 24: satellite dish (Constantine
Androsoff); 16: handcuffs (bg_knight); 22: security
camera (Kirill R); 26: missile (mmaxer); 28: gas mask
(VR Photos); 30: dynamite (Andrey Burmakin); 32:
bullets (Olemac); 36: megaphone (MilousSK); 40, 42:
handshake (David Gilder).

Every attempt has been made to clear copyright.
Should there be any inadvertent omission, please apply
to the publisher for rectification.

CONTENTS

A NEW KIND OF WAR

The war on terror began on September 11, 2001 in the United States. The day began as usual. Commuters made their way to work. Fifty thousand people entered the twin towers of New York's World Trade Center. In Washington, DC, workers arrived at the Pentagon, headquarters of the US Department of Defense. Flights 11 and 175 took off from Boston, Flight 77 from Washington, and Flight 93 from Newark.

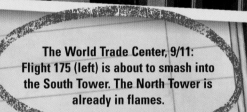

The World Trade Center, 9/11: Flight 175 (left) is about to smash into the South Tower. The North Tower is already in flames.

TERROR FROM THE SKIES

Just before 8:45 a.m., New Yorkers watched in horror as a Boeing 767 (Flight 11) hit the North Tower of the World Trade Center. At 9:03, Flight 175 hit the South Tower. At 9:40, Flight 77 crashed into the Pentagon. Flight 93 crashed in Pennsylvania. It never reached its target—probably the White House.

ISLAMISTS

Islamists are Muslim extremists who believe in a very strict interpretation of Islam. They see Islam not only as a religion but also as a political movement. They believe Muslims should unite politically. Islamists are hostile to Western influence in the Islamic world. Some of them are prepared to use force against those who oppose them.

The planes had been hijacked by terrorists. The terrorists had taken over the controls and then deliberately flown the planes into buildings full of people. They were linked to al-Qaeda, an Islamist group (see panel). September 11—9/11—was a day few forgot. This was a new kind of war.

SECRET WAR

Terrorism is not new—many countries, including Israel, Spain, and Britain, have suffered terrorist campaigns. But 9/11 was on a different scale. In response to the attacks, President George W. Bush declared a "war on terror."

Terrorist attacks are public events. By contrast, the war on terror is largely fought in secret. The fighters include soldiers, police, and secret agents—spies. It's a war of traps and tricks, fought with secret weapons, from robot planes to electronic spies.

IN THEIR OWN WORDS

After the 9/11 attacks, President Bush declared:

Make no mistake, the United States will hunt down and punish those responsible for these cowardly acts. Freedom itself was attacked this morning by a faceless coward. And freedom will be defended.

President George W. Bush, talking to the press at Barkdale Air Force Base, Louisiana, September 11, 2001

AFTER 9/11

The 9/11 attacks killed almost 3,000 people. Suspicion fell on al-Qaeda. This terrorist group had set off a truck bomb at the World Trade Center in 1993. In 1998, it bombed US embassies in Kenya and Tanzania. In 2000, al-Qaeda suicide bombers in Aden, Yemen, attacked the warship USS *Cole*.

OSAMA BIN LADEN

Osama bin Laden was born in 1957. In the 1980s, he went to Afghanistan to help fight the Soviet Union, which had invaded the country in 1979. In about 1988, he formed al-Qaeda ("the base"). Bin Laden wants to rid Muslim countries of Western influence, impose Sharia (strict Islamic) law, and create a unified Islamic world. Since 9/11, he has evaded all attempts at capture by Coalition forces. He is thought to be somewhere in the lawless region on the border of Afghanistan and Pakistan.

After 2001, Osama bin Laden sent audio and video messages from secret hideouts. This picture of the al-Qaeda leader was taken somewhere in Afghanistan.

THE TALIBAN AND AL-QAEDA

Investigators identified 19 suicide terrorists who had taken part in 9/11. The trail led to Afghanistan. In 2001, Afghanistan was ruled by an Islamist movement called the Taliban. They had seized the country in 1996 and had turned Afghanistan into an Islamist state with strict religious laws.

The Taliban provided a base for Saudi Arabian–born terrorist Osama bin Laden and his movement, al-Qaeda. Bin Laden set up training camps for al-Qaeda fighters in Afghanistan. The 9/11 attacks were almost certainly planned there.

WAR IN AFGHANISTAN

On September 14, 2001 the United States named bin Laden as the chief suspect for 9/11. President Bush demanded that the Taliban hand over the al-Qaeda leader. The Taliban refused. On October 7, 2001 a US-led coalition invaded Afghanistan. By December, the Taliban had been overthrown. A new government was formed, but the Taliban kept fighting. By 2009, more than 40 nations were taking part in the coalition fighting the Taliban for control of Afghanistan.

IN THEIR OWN WORDS

President George W. Bush first used the term "war on terror" in a speech to Congress on September 20, 2001:

Our war on terror begins with al-Qaeda, but it does not end there. It will not end until every terrorist group of global reach has been found, stopped, and defeated.

TERROR CELLS

Following the invasion of Afghanistan, al-Qaeda bases and training camps were destroyed. Osama bin Laden and the surviving al-Qaeda leadership fled Afghanistan. The movement dispersed and continued its terror war by means of secret, virtually independent cells around the world.

In 2007, an Islamist terrorist cell in Germany was uncovered by police. Three Germans and a Turk were accused of plotting bomb attacks against US and other Western targets.

SECRET NETWORKS

A cell is a small unit that forms part of a network. Each cell in the network operates independently but shares a common goal and vision with the other cells. The cell network has proved a useful form of organization for al-Qaeda because it is harder for counterterrorist agencies to penetrate it. One cell might be destroyed, but because each cell operates independently, the remaining cells can continue to function.

IN THEIR OWN WORDS

In December 2001, Osama bin Laden talked about the cell that planned and executed the 9/11 attacks:

Mohamed [Atta] from the Egyptian family [cell] was in charge of the group . . . The brothers [cell members], all they know is that they have a martyrdom operation.

From a videotape broadcast on al-Jazeera TV, Dec 14, 2001

Cell members are given only the minimum of information about the rest of the network so if they are captured, they cannot expose other cells or members. Communication between cells is done in secret by messengers and encrypted (coded) e-mails. Members may be watched by security forces, so they use false names and stolen passports. They change addresses frequently.

RECRUITMENT AND FINANCE

Cells recruit new members at workplaces, youth clubs, or mosques. Recruits are shown training videos about "jihad," or holy war. They are taught about Islamist religious and political beliefs. Some are taught how to use weapons and bombs. Other cell members are responsible for raising funds. They may do this by seeking donations from sympathetic individuals and organizations, or they may turn to crime—robbing banks, for example, or smuggling drugs.

JIHAD

Jihad is a word that appears frequently in the Islamic holy book, the Koran. It means "struggle in the way of God." Some Islamists have defined the word to mean a "holy war" against non-Muslims. They use it as a justification for terrorist attacks. According to the Koran, Islam may be spread "by the heart, the tongue, the hand, and the sword." Muslim scholars argue that terrorists who use only "the sword" (violence and war) disobey this teaching.

11

INTELLIGENCE NETWORKS

The armies in the war on terror are intelligence agencies. Their soldiers are secret agents or spies, police officers, code breakers, informers, and experts in many different skills, including languages and information technology. Most countries have a secret service. Examples are the US Central Intelligence Agency (CIA), Britain's Secret Intelligence Service (SIS), and Russia's SVR. These agencies often work together to fight terrorism.

Intelligence staff scan the media and the Internet 24/7 to uncover terror plots.

GATHERING INTELLIGENCE

Every report or rumor about terrorist activity is a piece of intelligence. This may come from a spy, another agency, or a member of the public. Intelligence gatherers check newspapers, radio, and TV in dozens of language for clues.

TERROR WATCH

The Federal Bureau of Investigation (FBI) leads the fight against terrorists within the United States. It works with the Department for Homeland Security, state police, and other agencies. The FBI screens travelers and watches out for "homegrown" terrorists. It runs a 24/7 call center for the public to call in to report any suspicious activity. Its website lists the "most-wanted terrorists."

PAKISTAN'S ISI

Pakistan is a Muslim country bordering Afghanistan. Terrorists have used Pakistan as a base, so Pakistan's Inter-Services Intelligence (ISI) is on the front line of the war on terror. Following 9/11, Pakistan decided to support the US-led invasion of Afghanistan. The ISI began to assist Western intelligence agencies by providing them with information on terrorist plots. The ISI is very powerful within Pakistani politics, and some have questioned its support for the war on terror. The CIA has accused members of the ISI of tipping off Taliban militants about Coalition attacks on them.

Four alleged spies arrested by Indian police in 2009. Indians with "terrorist backgrounds," supposedly hired by Pakistan's Inter-Services Intelligence, the spies were caught with photos, maps, phone contacts, and fake money.

Security officers at ports and airports pass on information about terrorist suspects on the move. Thousands of analysts work day and night listening to or reading satellite intercepts of phone calls or Internet exchanges between terrorist suspects.

CHECKING AND ANALYZING

Wherever it comes from, intelligence is studied carefully, recorded, and, if necessary, acted on. Intelligence may be what someone has seen: *Terrorist suspect Mr. A. has just arrived in London.* The report must be checked: Is it true? Is this really Mr. A.? Is the witness reliable? It must be analyzed: Is Mr. A. important? It may be passed on: *Tell New York Mr. A. is heading their way.* Or swift action may be taken: *Pick up Mr. A.*

MOLES AND INFORMERS

A mole is an undercover agent. In the war on terror, undercover agents may be used to infiltrate terrorist cells. Terrorists may also plant moles within government, military, or intelligence organizations to gather secrets. The mole does nothing to arouse suspicion. The more he or she is trusted, the more secrets a mole can pass on to a "contact." Some moles stay inactive for years as "sleepers" who are then "awakened" by a secret signal.

MUBIN SHAIKH

In November 2005, Canadian Muslim Mubin Shaikh joined a Toronto-based Islamist terror cell, telling its members he firmly believed in jihad. He helped to procure weapons for the cell and train its members in their use. In fact, Shaikh was a mole working for the Canadian secret service. His evidence would later help to bring down the "Toronto 17" terrorist cell.

The chief of police of the Philippines hands $10,000 to an informer, who is hooded to protect his identity. Some informers are offered protection and new identities.

LOOKING THE PART

Agents trying to infiltrate a terrorist cell have to look the part. They have to pretend to be a terrorist. They must have a good "cover story." Once inside the cell, their job is to identify leaders, discover plots, and foil attacks.

A MOLE AT SEA

In 2001, the USS *Benfold* was on patrol in the Persian Gulf. One of the warship's crew was Hassan Abu-Jihaad. Unknown to his shipmates, he was a mole, passing secrets to al-Qaeda. In 2003, British agents raided an al-Qaeda apartment. They found a computer disk sent by Abu-Jihaad. The FBI bugged his phone calls. Abu-Jihaad was arrested.

Al-Qaeda mole Abu-Jihaad was a crewman aboard the US destroyer USS *Benfold*, the lead ship in this photo.

PASSING ON SECRETS

Informers are people who were once part of terrorist cells and who then pass on information about their former comrades. An informer may have a grudge against other members. Informers can also be suspicious friends or relatives of terrorist cell members. In 2001, Youssef Hmimssa shared an apartment with a member of an al-Qaeda terrorist cell based in Detroit. In the wake of the 9/11 attacks, he informed the authorities about the cell. His evidence helped convict the four members of the cell in August 2002.

Some informers sell their information for money. An agent has to judge whether the informer is being truthful or just spinning a tale for a few dollars. Informers' identities are usually kept secret or changed for their own protection.

TERROR AND TORTURE

Once in captivity, a terrorist suspect can be interrogated for information about terrorist cells, plots, and networks. In some countries ruled by repressive regimes, torture and execution of terrorist suspects is routine. Most Western democratic countries no longer execute convicted criminals or terrorists. However, torture is sometimes used as part of an interrogation— although it is officially illegal.

BATTLEFIELD DETAINEES

Under the international rules of war, called the Geneva Conventions, a prisoner of war (POW) has certain rights, including being treated humanely. However, President Bush's administration claimed that al-Qaeda fighters captured in Afghanistan were not POWs but "battlefield detainees" and so not entitled to protection under the Geneva Conventions. Al-Qaeda suspects were placed in the US detention camp at Guantánamo Bay, Cuba.

Camp X-Ray, Guantánamo Bay: detainees in orange jumpsuits are guarded by US military police.

KHALID SHEIKH MOHAMMED

In 2003, senior member of al-Qaeda Khalid Sheikh Mohammed was captured in Pakistan and flown to Guantánamo Bay. In 2006, he claimed he had been tortured, including being subjected to "waterboarding." He said he provided a lot of false information that he thought the interrogators wanted to hear just to stop the torture.

This mystery plane at Prague airport, Czech Republic, in 2005, was said to be making extraordinary rendition flights, transporting terrorist suspects to other countries for interrogation using torture.

GUANTÁNAMO BAY

Some detainees at Guantánamo Bay claimed they were tortured. One torture was "waterboarding"—pouring water over a prisoner's face to induce a feeling of drowning. Others alleged they were tortured with broken glass, barbed wire and burning cigarettes. A 2007 FBI report detailed other forms of torture carried out at the detention camp. These included being chained hand and foot in a fetal position for 18 hours or more and being subjected to extremes of heat and cold.

EXTRAORDINARY RENDITION

Some journalists and human rights groups have claimed that the US government has bypassed its own laws against the use of torture by flying prisoners to other countries for torture. In a process known as extraordinary rendition, the CIA allegedly flew hundreds of terrorist suspects to countries such as Egypt, Jordan, Syria, and Morocco to be tortured. Information obtained under torture was then passed to the CIA. Within days of taking office in January 2009, the new president, Barack Obama, ended extraordinary rendition and announced plans to close the Guantánamo Bay detention camp.

IN THEIR OWN WORDS

We will not win the battle against this global extremism, unless we win it at the level of values as much as force, unless we show we are even-handed.

Tony Blair (British prime minister 1997–2007) interviewed in the *Times*, August 2, 2006

HOW TERRORISTS COMMUNICATE

Terrorist cells within al-Qaeda find secretive ways of communicating with each other, with other cells, and with the outside world. Communication is necessary to spread propaganda, to recruit new members, for training, and to plan and coordinate attacks.

CODES

Terrorists often use encrypted messages—messages in code. Only the person receiving the message knows the code key and so is able to read the message. A simple code may replace one type of symbol with another—numbers for letters, for example. The codes that are hardest to break make use of obscure words or a language that few outsiders speak well.

Terrorism uses the World Wide Web: an alleged al-Qaeda member sends an encrypted message via the Internet. This image appeared on a video obtained by the CNN TV network.

NEW AND OLD TECHNOLOGY

The great advances in communications technology since 1990 have allowed an organization such as al-Qaeda to operate on a global scale. E-mail, fax, cell phones, and satellite phones allow rapid communication between locations thousands of miles apart.

However, the new technology is a double-edged sword: messages can be intercepted, monitored, and traced to particular phones or computers. Even encrypted (coded) messages can often be cracked by talented code breakers. As a result, terrorists now frequently rely on old-fashioned couriers. Couriers memorize messages in case they are captured.

THE INTERNET

The Internet has big advantages for terrorists. It is difficult to censor or shut down, if sites are shut down, new ones can easily be created, and messages can be sent anonymously, quickly, and cheaply. Since the loss of their Afghan base in 2002, al-Qaeda has used the Internet as a "virtual base" to continue communicating with its fighters and followers. Online training manuals show recruits how to make booby traps, poisoned letters, letter bombs, and phones that detonate bombs. Al-Qaeda also uses the Internet for planning operations, intelligence gathering, and fund raising.

Video footage shown on Al-Jazeera TV of Osama bin Laden (right) and the number two in al-Qaeda, Ayman al-Zawahiri. Intelligence analysts study such images for clues as to their whereabouts.

HUMINT AND SIGINT

Counterterrorist agencies use two main types of intelligence. HUMINT is "human intelligence," gathered from human sources such as moles, informers, and witnesses. SIGINT, or "signals intelligence," comes from monitoring the airwaves—radio, phone calls, and e-mails. Analysts study the "raw intelligence" gathered by SIGINT and HUMINT—these are the "dots." The analysts' job is to join up the dots to form a more complete picture of terrorist activity.

ELECTRONIC EYES AND EARS

Millions of international phone calls are made via satellite every day. In the wake of the 9/11 attacks, the US government launched the Terrorist Surveillance Program to intercept those calls where one of the parties is a suspected terrorist. The aim was to gather intelligence about terrorist cells and possible new terrorist plots.

The domes at Royal Air Force (RAF) Menwith Hill, United Kingdom, hide scanners that eavesdrop on electronic communications, gathering intelligence about terrorist activity.

COMMUNICATIONS CENTERS

The electronic eyes and ears of the war on terror are communications centers, where the satellite intercepts are analyzed by human experts and computers. Two such centers are the US National Security Agency headquarters at Fort Meade in Maryland and RAF Menwith Hill in Yorkshire, England.

COMPUTER ENCRYPTION

Encryption changes "plain text" into code, using algorithms (rules used for solving math problems) or ciphers (substitution of symbols in accordance with a system). Terrorists use encryption codes to protect their computer data from counterterrorist agents. Computer encryption and code breaking is a continuing battle of wits, and software, between terrorists and trackers.

Phone tapping can provide evidence of terrorist activity. Such evidence is allowed in the courts of many, though not all, countries.

PHONE TAPS

Security services keep lists of the phone numbers of terrorist suspects so that if a suspect makes a call, it can be intercepted. These are called "red-flag" numbers. Phones can be tapped by using an IMSI catcher (IMSI stands for International Mobile Subscriber Identity). This device pretends to be part of a phone network but intercepts calls. Agents call this a "man in the middle attack." Caller and receiver never know they're being listened to.

In Pakistan, all calls pass through a "listening room" at the Counterterrorism Center. Calls from "red-flag" numbers are traced by direction finder. The callers are arrested or tracked to see what they are up to.

SCREEN PEEKING AND WALL GAZING

Spies can peek into a terrorist suspect's room and read his or her e-mails. Using an infrared laser beam camera-telescope, agents can look at the suspect's eyeball. In it, they can see the reflections from a computer screen. Brick walls can't keep the agents out either. With a "sense through the wall" Xaver (which uses radar to look through walls) agents can see who is behind locked doors.

TRACK AND TRACE

Terrorists often steal identities in order to remain undetected while traveling, communicating, and interracting with others. They steal personal data, passports, drivers' licenses, and identity cards. However, new biometric passports are encoded with each person's unique face, fingerprint, and eye details and are much harder to fake.

9/11 terrorists Mohamed Atta (right) and Abdulaziz al-Omari are recorded on a security camera at the Portland airport, Maine, just hours before the 2001 attacks on the United States.

CYBER-SPIES

Using the latest computer-monitoring technology, spies can open "security holes" in computer systems. Their scanners can "listen in" to a printer and translate the clicks into words. Or they can pick up the radio waves from a computer monitor and the signals from a video cable and convert this into information. With a webcam and smart software, a spy can record a suspect's fingers tapping on a keyboard and work out what the suspect is typing.

TRAVELER'S CHECKS

In 2000, Mohamed Atta, leader of the 9/11 terrorists, found it easy to enter the United States. He even took a pilot-training course in Florida as he planned the attack on New York's World Trade Center. All of this would be harder now. The US Federal Aviation Administration checks tickets and passenger lists. Other countries run similar checks.

At airports, people and bags are scanned. In 2001, terrorist Richard Reid hid a bomb in his shoe—he was caught before he could explode it on the plane. Now even shoes have to be removed as part of the screening process.

Biometric scanners check travelers' identities. This passenger at JFK International Airport, New York, is having his thumbprint checked by US Homeland Security.

WATCH THE CAMERA

To track and trace suspects, images from CCTV (closed-circuit television) cameras can be useful. These cameras record crowds in stores, airports, and train and bus stations. Still photos taken from CCTV footage can then be analyzed using facial recognition technology to try and match suspects to known terrorists.

Agents also make use of magnifying cameras to record images from safe distances. Such cameras can read a car license plate or identify a face from almost two miles (three kilometers) away. With a thermal imager (a camera that detects body heat), agents can look inside a building and see where the people are.

IN THEIR OWN WORDS

Terrorists . . . need places to live and work, and . . . train. Such places may be in remote areas . . . but they exist, can be found and will be hit.

John Keegan, British journalist, *Daily Telegraph*, September 13, 2001

23

SPIES IN SPACE

With a computer, anyone can Google up a satellite map or take a virtual stroll through city streets. This technology can also help terrorists. Both al-Qaeda and Hamas, a Palestinian Islamist group, have used Google Earth to plan attacks. But satellite technology gives counterterrorists an advantage too.

A spy satellite in Earth orbit can pinpoint terrorist training camps and secret weapon dumps. Other satellites monitor communications and guide security forces to targets.

WATCHING THE ENEMY

Spy satellites in orbit around the Earth are equipped with cameras capable of super-high magnification. They can take high-definition photographs of enemy activity in conflict zones such as Afghanistan—a convoy of trucks, say, or even two people meeting by a village well. The satellites also monitor the constant babble of radio, video, Internet, and phone traffic down below.

LOOKING FOR OSAMA BIN LADEN

After 9/11, US military spy satellites were assigned the task of hunting down Osama bin Laden. They still watch and listen, relaying pictures and video footage from drone planes flying above the mountains where he might be hiding. Satellites also send map details to guide the soldiers trekking over rough ground in search of their elusive enemy.

SHADOW SPYING

Because satellites are always above the subjects of their photographs, they are not great at identification since they usually only show the top of a person's head. However, a satellite can also photograph shadows. Shadows show the way we walk, and we all walk in an individual way. Terrorists can alter their appearance by wearing a disguise or by plastic surgery, but they can't disguise the way they walk.

NASA (the US space agency) has new software that can recognize a person's walk from their shadow. If that person's walk is on file, an identification match can be made. Intelligence agencies keep millions of face photos on file. From now on, they will video people's walks too. Matching shadow walks from space could help find missing terrorists.

KEYHOLE SATELLITES

US "keyhole" (KH) satellites are orbiting digital cameras with extra-powerful zooms. They can "peep through keyholes" to spot an object a mere six inches (15 centimeters) long. That is like seeing someone's shoe from over 186 miles (300 kilometers) above the Earth! Images from these satellites are studied at the US National Geospatial-Intelligence Agency (NGA). The NGA provides valuable data for soldiers fighting in Afghanistan and for the intelligence services hunting terrorists.

KABUL RADCOM STATION NORTHWEST, AFGHANISTAN
PRE STRIKE

A satellite image shows a communications base near Kabul, one of many Taliban targets picked out for attack by planners before the 2001 invasion of Afghanistan.

SPY PLANES AND DRONES

In conventional wars, helicopters, bombers, and fighters are in the thick of combat. In the secret war against the terrorists, spy planes and drones circle like birds of prey. They watch and track, and sometimes strike.

The MQ-9 Reaper, a bigger version of the Predator UAV, has been used in Afghanistan since 2007. Driven by a rear propeller, the Reaper fires up to 12 missiles.

VACUUM CLEANER IN THE SKY

The propeller-powered EP-3E looks like an elderly airliner. Its secrets are in its electronics. It "sucks up" e-communications (phone calls, e-mails, faxes, and satellite signals). No wonder it's called "the vacuum cleaner in the sky." Most of its crew of 24 watch scanners and radar screens as the plane flies on 12-hour patrols.

BIRD'S-EYE VIEW

Airborne command centers, such as the big AWACS aircraft with their radar domes, give generals a "bird's-eye view" of military operations. They direct troops and bombers to targets. Other planes are spies in the sky, photographing enemy bases and intercepting their communications.

UNMANNED AIRCRAFT

Even a fast jet can be shot down by a missile from the ground. To save pilots' lives, the army uses unmanned aerial vehicles (UAVs)—planes without pilots—such as the Predator and Reaper drones. A UAV can fly itself by computer or be guided by a controller at a desk thousands of miles away. It flies slowly and often at high altitudes. Its scanners can detect the ground even through clouds or sandstorms.

A drone's brain is the electronics in its nose cone. Some of this gear scans the ground below. Some sends messages to satellites in space. The satellites pass on images and overheard radio conversations from the drone to its controllers.

KILLER DRONE

Drones also carry Hellfire missiles. From June 2009, drones were increasingly used in an offensive role against Taliban forces in northwest Pakistan. In August 2009, a Predator's missile killed Baitullah Mehsud, the Taliban commander in Pakistan.

MAVS

Micro air vehicles (MAVs) are tiny, remote-controlled aircraft with wingspans of about six inches (15 centimeters). They are currently being developed for use in the war on terror as spies and scouts. Fixed wing MAVs can fly long distances, but rotary wing (helicopter) MAVs are better able to enter buildings since they are able to hover and make tight turns. For the more distant future, engineers are working on insect-size MAVs.

SECRET WEAPONS

Both sides in the war on terror use secret weapons. The terrorist hunters use hitech weapons such as drones and spy satellites. The terrorists use homemade bombs and keep changing the way they make them to fool bomb-disposal experts.

Improvised explosive devices (IEDs) are set off by remote control. This bomb in the Gaza Strip, hidden beneath the road, was detonated as an Israeli bulldozer drove past.

GUNS, BOMBS, AND MISSILES

Terrorists trade and smuggle guns and missiles around the world. Some are stolen from government stockpiles; others are made in secret factories. A bomb can be made in a shed using store-bought chemicals—fertilizer, for example. Bombs can be made by following step-by-step instructions on terrorist websites. In March 2004, al-Qaeda terrorists used cell phones to detonate bombs on four trains in Madrid, Spain, killing 191 people. The terrorists built the bombs using instructions downloaded from the Internet.

WEAPONS OF MASS DESTRUCTION

Weapons of mass destruction (WMD) are biological, chemical, or nuclear weapons. Biological weapons spread deadly bacteria, such as smallpox or anthrax. In 2001 a terrorist sent anthrax spores through the US mail to news offices and two senators. Five people died.

Chemical weapons deliver toxic substances such as chlorine or mustard gas. Poison gas attacks are fortunately very rare. One reason is that killer chemicals such as sarin can be just as dangerous to the terrorists as to their victims.

Nuclear weapons are bombs with massive explosive power caused by the splitting of the nuclei of atoms. Those not killed in the explosion could die from radiation sickness caused by the cloud of radioactive dust left behind. Nuclear weapons are hard to make, but terrorists may be able to create radiological weapons, or "dirty bombs." These are conventional bombs packed with radioactive material, which scatters when the bomb goes off.

In this training exercise, a US firefighter in protective gear checks a "victim" for radioactivity, following a simulated nuclear attack on Los Angeles.

POISON GAS

In 1995, the Japanese terrorist group Aum Shinrikyo used a poison gas called sarin in an attack on the Tokyo subway. Sarin is deadly. A pinhead droplet of the gas can kill a person. Twelve people died in the Tokyo attack, and thousands were injured.

29

SUICIDE ATTACKS

A suicide attack kills both attacker and victims. Suicide bombers carry their explosives in a car or truck or on a belt or vest hidden under clothing. Some carry their bomb in a backpack. Suicide attacks are particularly dangerous because the bomber can control the exact position and timing of the blast— in a crowded street or subway, for example—to cause the maximum number of casualties.

21ST-CENTURY WEAPON

Suicide attacks are not new. During World War II, Japanese kamikaze pilots flew their planes into US warships. However, the frequency of suicide attacks has greatly increased in recent years. Almost 75 percent of all suicide attacks have taken place since 9/11, which was itself a suicide attack. There have been nearly a thousand suicide attacks in Iraq since the US-led invasion in 2003. In Afghanistan, the Taliban began using suicide attacks after 2006 as they lost ground on the battlefield.

Ali Imron, jailed for the Bali bombings of 2002, shows police a mock suicide bomb vest, with explosives hidden in pockets. The Bali bombers used this type of vest and also a car bomb to blow up a nightclub.

A Palestinian suicide bomber blew up this bus in the Israeli city of Haifa in 2003. The bomber was one of the bus passengers. As rescue workers remove casualties, police hunt for clues among the wreckage.

Suicide attacks were frequently used during the Palestinian uprising against Israel (2000–2005), especially by the Palestinian Islamist group Hamas. Suicide bombers have also targeted Westerners. Backpack bombers were responsible for the the Bali nightclub bombings (2002), the Madrid train bombings (2004), and the London bombings on July 7, 2005.

GRUESOME EVIDENCE

After a suicide attack, police carefully examine every scrap of wreckage for clues. Bits of bomb casing may show where the bomb was made. Doctors examine body parts to try to identify victims and bomber. A shattered face can be "rebuilt" by surgeons and computer experts. The face of a dead bomber may match a photo on file. That photo, and a name, may lead to a terrorist cell and another small victory in the war against terror.

MARTYRS?

Suicide bombers often leave videos of themselves. They say goodbye to families and friends. They call themselves martyrs, ready to die for their beliefs. However, in Islamic teaching, a true martyr (*shahid*) dies fighting in a jihad, or holy war. Many Islamic teachers point out that suicide is against the Prophet Mohammed's teaching. The Koran also forbids the killing of innocent civilians.

31

ASSASSINS AND HOSTAGE TAKERS

In December 2007, a suicide attacker—probably a member of al-Qaeda—assassinated Benazir Bhutto while she was campaigning for election in Pakistan. She was seen as pro-Western by many Islamists. Assassination is the killing of someone for political reasons. Terrorists use assassination to remove enemies—usually political leaders—or to shock or intimidate governments.

Mourners light candles for murdered Pakistani leader Benazir Bhutto, 2007.

HIGH-VALUE TARGETS

Security forces also use assassination as a tool in the war on terror. Terrorist or enemy leaders are known as high-value targets (HVTs). In May 2007, special forces in Afghanistan hunted down Taliban leader Mullah Dadullah. A helicopter flew in assault troops, who killed Mullah Dadullah, along with 20 Taliban fighters.

KILLING BY CAMERA

Ahmed Shah Massoud was a mujahideen general in Afghanistan. He was one of the leaders of the Northern Alliance (a group of armies fighting the Taliban). Massoud was murdered only days before the 9/11 attacks. Al-Qaeda killed him to win friends among the Taliban. Two Arab "journalists" came to interview him. Their camera was a bomb. When they got close to Massoud, they detonated it, killing him and themselves.

HOSTAGES

A hostage is a person kidnapped and held captive for a ransom. Kidnappers usually demand money or the freeing of comrades in jail. If their demands are not met, they kill the hostage.

Hostage taking is effective because it gets plenty of media attention, which the terrorists try to use to gain publicity for their cause. It also appears to place responsibility for the hostage's life in the hands of the enemy. By placing pressure on the enemy to negotiate, hostage taking can give terrorists—for a short time at least—a feeling of power and status.

In the mid-2000s, Islamist hostage takers frequently posted videos of hostages on the Internet. Some showed them pleading for their lives; others showed them being killed.

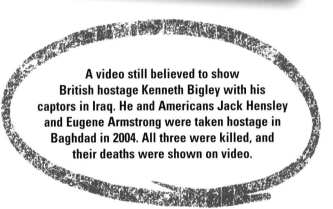

A video still believed to show British hostage Kenneth Bigley with his captors in Iraq. He and Americans Jack Hensley and Eugene Armstrong were taken hostage in Baghdad in 2004. All three were killed, and their deaths were shown on video.

IN THEIR OWN WORDS

Kenneth Bigley, who was held hostage in Iraq by the Islamist group Tawhid and Jihad, appealed to British prime minister Tony Blair for help in a video made by the hostage takers. Bigley was killed shortly afterwards.

I need you to help me now, Mr. Blair, because you are the only person on God's earth who can help me.

From a video posted on an Islamist website, September 22, 2004

33

SPECIAL FORCES IN COMBAT

Special forces are trained for secret and dangerous missions. Most armies have them. Examples are the US Navy SEALS (Sea, Air, and Land forces) and SOAR (Special Operations Aviation Regiment) and the British SAS (Special Air Service) and SBS (Special Boat Service).

A British Royal Marine in Afghanistan takes up a defensive position while waiting to be "extracted"— airlifted out of a danger zone by a Chinook helicopter.

MISSIONS

Special forces soldiers do reconnaissance (scouting and intelligence gathering), attack enemy command posts, and mark targets for aircraft to bomb. They are trained to live off the land and sleep in the open. They can find their way across mountains and deserts using GPS (Global Positioning System) navigation equipment. They contact headquarters by radio, using a satellite link and foldaway dish aerials.

IN THEIR OWN WORDS

Petty Officer Marcus Luttrell of the Navy SEALs received the Navy Cross for his actions in 2005 facing Taliban fighters during a special forces operation in Afghanistan. He later commented:

We don't habitually get captured. Either we kill our enemy or our enemy kills us. SEALs don't put their hands up waving white flags. Period.

A special forces mission may begin with a night flight in a helicopter or a bumpy ride in a Humvee bristling with missile launchers and machine guns. Special forces soldiers travel in small groups. Some dress in heavily camouflaged military uniforms. Others wear local clothing so they can blend into civilian populations.

WEAPONS AND GEAR

Special forces weapons are often customized. A regular US M4A1 carbine (rifle) has extras such as see-in-the-dark sights, a laser target illuminator, and a silencer. Soldiers may carry sniper rifles, pistols, grenades, and anti-tank missiles. They may use an AK-47 assault rifle. This Russian weapon is also often used by terrorists because it is simple and reliable.

Night-vision aids give special forces troops an edge when fighting in the dark. They wear infrared reflective arm patches to distinguish friend from foe at night. Each soldier carries food, water, a survival kit, and a sleeping bag in a pack that weighs over 165 pounds (75 kilograms).

NAVY SEAL HERO

On March 2, 2002, a SOAR unit was piloting a team of Navy SEALs over the mountain of Takur Ghar, Afghanistan, in a Chinook helicopter when a rocket-propelled grenade struck the side of the craft. The helicopter managed to escape, but one SEAL, Neil Roberts, was thrown from the craft and fell to the snowy ground. He immediately engaged al-Qaeda forces with a pistol and two grenades. He survived for at least 30 minutes before being shot and killed.

US Navy SEAL Neil Roberts, age 32, is one of many who have served and died in Afghanistan. After falling from his helicopter during a mission, he was killed on the ground fighting al-Qaeda.

PROPAGANDA WARS

Propaganda is information or publicity put out by a government or organization to promote an idea or cause. One of the main goals of terrorism is propaganda. Terrorists want to show through violent action who they are and what they stand for. Italian revolutionary Carlo Pisacane (1818–1857) called this "propaganda of the deed."

MEDIA MANIPULATION

Terrorists have become very good at maximizing media coverage, which is why they bomb city centers at busy times of day. They know that the media will be unable to ignore such attacks.

Terrorist groups have become adept at using new technologies to advance their causes. Al-Qaeda produces DVDs and videos of sermons, battles, suicide attacks, and hostage beheadings to project its violent image to potential supporters. Some of these are shown on Arabic TV networks such as al-Jazeera or on video-sharing websites such as YouTube. Some

IN THEIR OWN WORDS

Mustafa Abu al-Yazid, self-proclaimed leader of al-Qaeda in Afghanistan, tried to inspire his followers in a propaganda video released in 2007:

Your hero sons, courageous knights have left to the land of Afghanistan . . . the land of jihad and martyrdom, answering the call for the sake of God to kick out the occupier who has desecrated the pure soil of Afghanistan.

terrorist groups such as Hezbollah (an Islamist group based in Lebanon) even have their own private television stations, giving them complete control over how their message is presented.

WINNING HEARTS AND MINDS

Governments also use propaganda to win hearts and minds in the terror war. During the 2001 invasion of Afghanistan, Coalition aircraft beamed radio messages in local Afghan languages. They dropped leaflets saying the Taliban were criminals and informing people of the $25 million reward for Osama bin Laden. Northern Alliance leader General Dostum joined in on Afghan radio: "This is General Dostum speaking. I am here and I have brought the Americans with me."

TERRORIST OR FREEDOM FIGHTER?

Governments tend to apply the blanket term "terrorist" to their enemies in the war on terror, but is this in itself a form of propaganda? Terrorists rarely refer to themselves as such. They call themselves freedom fighters, revolutionaries, or jihadis. Defining these people by their actions (terrorism) rather than by their cause is arguably a form of propaganda.

STATE-SPONSORED TERRORISM

Terrorists sometimes receive support from governments. This is known as state-sponsored terrorism. It enables terrorists to mount operations they could not fund themselves, and it allows governments to damage their enemies without having to risk open warfare. States provide terrorist groups with funds, weapons, materials, and secure areas where they can plan operations and train recruits.

TERRORIST SAFE HAVENS

In addition to receiving support from certain governments, terrorists make use of states or regions where the government is weak or nonexistent. These lawless or semi-lawless places provide safe havens from which terrorists can organize, plan, raise funds, communicate, recruit, and train in relative security. They include Somalia in East Africa and the Afghan-Pakistan border. Lebanon in the Middle East, despite support from UN forces, remains another haven for terrorists.

Militia patrol the streets of Mogadishu, capital of Somalia. This semi-lawless nation, devastated by a long civil war, has become a haven for Islamist terrorist groups.

Sudan's Sadiq al-Mahdi, a political and religious leader, meets Khaled Mashal, head of the militant Palestinian group Hamas. Sudan is accused of being a "safe haven" for extremists.

AMERICAN LIST

In 2009, the US State Department listed the following countries as state sponsors of terrorism: Cuba, Iran, Syria, and Sudan. The United States banned arms-related exports to those countries and refused them economic aid.

CUBA

Cuba has not actively supported terrorism for many years, but according to the State Department continues to provide a safe haven for several known South American terrorists.

IRAN

Iran is probably the world's most active state sponsor of terrorism. The Quds Force, a branch of Iran's Islamic Revolutionary Guard Corps, provides weapons, training, and funding to a number of Islamist groups, including Hamas, Hezbollah, Iraqi militants, and the Taliban.

SYRIA

Syria is also an active supporter of terrorist organizations such as Hamas, Hezbollah, and other Palestinian and Iraqi militant groups. Some Hezbollah and Hamas leaders have made their bases in the Syrian capital Damascus. While publicly condemning terrorism, Syria regards groups such as Hamas as freedom fighters rather than terrorists.

SUDAN

Sudan has played on both sides of the conflict. While supporting the global counterterrorism effort, it continues to give safe haven to Islamist groups such as Hamas and Palestine Islamic Jihad. It seems powerless to prevent al-Qaeda cells from operating within its borders.

IN THEIR OWN WORDS

If the Afghanistan government falls to the Taliban or allows al-Qaeda to go unchallenged, that country will again be a base of terrorists . . .

President Barack Obama, from a speech on March 27, 2009, announcing a "comprehensive new strategy for Afghanistan"

SECRET DEALS

The war on terror poses difficult questions for governments. Should they respond with an aggressively military strategy, adding to the bloodshed and possibly creating more converts to the terrorists' cause—or should they try talking to the terrorists? The idea of negotiating with terrorists is distasteful to many, particularly those who have lost loved ones in terrorist attacks. However, governments do talk to terrorists, although they don't always like to publicize the fact.

A South Korean hostage freed by the Taliban in Afghanistan, with Red Cross officials. In 2007, the Taliban took 23 Koreans hostage, killing two before the South Korean government made a deal.

TALKING WITH THE TALIBAN

In November 2008, General David McKiernan, then commander of US forces in Afghanistan, was among the first to suggest publicly the possibility of negotiating with the Taliban. He distinguished Taliban with a small *t*— those who fight for food, fear or inter-tribal reasons—and capital *T* Taliban, who fight for ideological reasons. He believed it was possible to win over the small *t* Taliban and isolate the extremists.

IN THEIR OWN WORDS

The idea of reconciliation at the local level of local fighters, of local influencers, potentially is a very powerful metric in Afghanistan.

General David McKiernan, speaking at the Atlantic Council of the United States in November 2008

The Pakistani government negotiated a deal with the Taliban in April 2009. Pakistan allowed the Taliban to establish Sharia (strict Islamic) law in the Swat Valley in northwest Pakistan in exchange for laying down their arms. The deal broke down in weeks, but it was the first sign of a new strategy of trying, where possible, to build bridges.

THE SUNNI AWAKENING

The strategy of negotiating with moderate elements within the enemy in order to isolate the extremists certainly worked in Iraq. In November 2005, US forces struck a deal with Sunni tribal leaders in Anbar Province, one of the most violent areas of Iraq since the 2003 US-led invasion. This led to the so-called "Sunni Awakening." The US military provided Sunni militias with weapons and training, and the Sunnis then turned on al-Qaeda fighters, who had a strong presence there.

Anbar soon became one of the safest places in Iraq. Similar deals were made with tribal leaders in many parts of the country, severely damaging al-Qaeda in Iraq and turning the tide of the Iraq War in favor of the Coalition.

"GOOD" AND "BAD" TALIBAN

Afghan elders did a deal with some "good" Taliban fighters in 2009 to reduce attacks during presidential elections. Coalition commanders hope more "good" Taliban will break away from the extremists and help to rebuild Afghanistan.

An Iraqi militiaman jokes with a US soldier during the 2005 "Sunni Awakening," which aimed to enlist local leaders and fighters to rise up against al-Qaeda militants in Iraq.

41

WAR WITH NO WINNERS?

Conventional wars between countries usually end when one or other side surrenders or when neither side wants to fight on and a peace agreement is made. The end of the war on terror is unlikely to be so clear cut.

Some Afghan Taliban have been ready to stop fighting. Here, an Afghan official hands over surrendered Taliban weapons to a United Nations representative.

CAN TERRORISM BE DEFEATED?

Some have argued that the whole concept of the war on terror is flawed because terrorism is a method, not a cause, and therefore cannot be fought or defeated. Certainly it is unlikely that terrorism will ever disappear entirely. So long as there remain groups within society willing to fight and die for a cause, there will always be terrorism. The best that can be hoped for is that the current upsurge in Islamist-inspired terrorism will gradually burn itself out.

Terrorism will almost certainly not be defeated by military means alone. Counterterrorism involves governments working together to disrupt terrorist financing and communications and to break up terrorist cells. It also involves listening to the concerns of young

Muslims who are likely to be swayed by the Islamist message. If Western governments adopt policies that are more sensitive to Muslim concerns, the Islamists will lose much of their appeal.

THE CHALLENGE

In waging war against suspected terrorists on the home front, governments must tread carefully. The use of CCTV, phone tapping, and imprisonment without trial affects the lives of all citizens, not just terrorists. If governments exploit the fear of terrorism to impose repressive laws, cherished freedoms may be threatened. The challenge is to defeat terrorism without losing those freedoms. Otherwise the war on terror will have no winners.

THE FUTURE IN AFGHANISTAN

The Coalition aims to bring peace and security to Afghanistan under a strong, stable government so that it can no longer act as a base for al-Qaeda to launch attacks on the West. To this end, in December 2009, President Obama decided to send 30,000 more troops to the region. This was intended as a short-term measure—Afghans would soon be expected to start taking charge of their own security. However, critics saw it as part of an escalation of a war that could last many more years.

Egypt's president Hosni Mubarak (left) greets President Barack Obama. During Obama's 2009 visit to Egypt, he made a keynote speech addressed to the Islamic world.

IN THEIR OWN WORDS

America is not, and never will be, at war with Islam. We will, however, relentlessly confront violent extremists who pose a grave threat to our security—because we reject the same thing that people of all faiths reject: the killing of innocent men, women, and children.

President Obama, from a speech he made in Egypt in June 2009

TIMELINE

February 23, 1998 Al-Qaeda declares war on the United States and its supporters.

September 11, 2001 The 9/11 attacks kill 3,000.

September 28, 2001 The United Nations Security Council passes Resolution 1373, calling on all nations to work together to fight terrorism.

October 7, 2001 Operation Enduring Freedom, the US-led invasion of Afghanistan, begins.

October 26, 2001 The US Patriot Act is passed, giving the government increased powers to search and arrest terrorist suspects.

January 11, 2002 The first detainees arrive at Guantánamo Bay detention camp.

May 8, 2002 Islamist Jose Padilla, trained in making a "dirty bomb" is arrested in Chicago.

August 28, 2002 Members of an al-Qaeda cell in Detroit are convicted on terrorism charges thanks to evidence from an informer.

October 14, 2002 Al-Qaeda terrorists bomb a nightclub in Bali, Indonesia, killing 200.

March 20, 2003 A US-led coalition invades Iraq.

March 11, 2004 Al-Qaeda terrorists bomb commuter trains in Madrid, killing 191.

October 7, 2004 Hostage Kenneth Bigley is killed by his captors, Tawhid and Jihad.

July 7, 2005 Al-Qaeda terrorists bomb underground trains and a bus in London, killing 56.

December 27, 2007 An al-Qaeda suicide bomber kills Pakistani politician Benazir Bhutto.

August 5, 2009 Baitullah Mehsud, the Taliban commander in Pakistan, is mortally wounded by a missile from an unmanned Predator drone.

December 25, 2009 An al-Qaeda suicide bomber, Umar Farouk Abdulmutallab, fails in his attempt to blow up a passenger plane.

GLOSSARY

al-Qaeda An Islamist terrorist network that has carried out numerous large-scale attacks, including 9/11.

CCTV Closed-circuit television. A surveillance system in which cameras transmit pictures by cable to connected monitors.

CIA Central Intelligence Agency. A bureau responsible for providing national security intelligence to senior US policy makers.

cipher A language or system used to translate a message into code or to decipher a coded message.

coalition An alliance of countries working and fighting together for a common purpose.

counterterrorism Military or political activities intended to combat or prevent terrorism.

courier A person who delivers messages.

democratic Describing a country in which the government is elected by the people.

dispersed Distributed or scattered.

drone A pilotless plane.

encryption The conversion of text or computer data into a code to prevent unauthorized people from gaining access to it.

extremist A person prepared to use extreme measures, including violence, to pursue his or her aims.

FBI Federal Bureau of Investigation, a department of the US Department of Justice that deals with matters of national security and crimes against the government.

fetal Curled up, like a fetus.

GPS Global positioning by satellite. Using a receiver to pick up signals transmitted by satellites, it is possible for a person to calculate his or her position on the ground.

intelligence Information, often secret, about an enemy's forces and plans.

intercept Pick up (for example, a radio transmission).

Islamist Someone who follows a strict form of Islam based on a literal interpretation of the Koran.

jihad The struggle for Islam. This can be interpreted either as a holy war or as a spiritual striving.

Koran The holy text of Islam.

martyr A person prepared to die for his or her religious beliefs.

militia A group of people who arm themselves and carry out military operations.

mujahideen Muslim guerrilla fighters.

Muslim A follower of Islam, the religion founded by the prophet Mohammed.

Northern Alliance A multi-ethnic alliance in Afghanistan who are united in their opposition to the Taliban.

nuclear weapon Bombs or missiles that release nuclear energy to create a massive explosion.

Sharia Islamic law.

sleeper A mole or secret agent who remains hidden and inactive, sometimes for years.

Sunni The largest branch of Islam—90 percent of all Muslims are Sunni. They follow the teachings handed down by the first caliphs, successors of the prophet Mohammed.

Taliban An Islamist militia that took over Afghanistan in 1996 and set up an Islamist state there. They have fought the government and Coalition troops since losing power in 2001.

thermal imager A device that detects a hidden person from body heat.

FURTHER INFORMATION

BOOKS
Barr, Gary. *Behind the News: War on Terror: Is the World Safer?* Heinemann, 2006.

Downing, David. *Timelines: The War on Terror*. Watts, 2007.

Jamieson, Alison. *Global Questions: Can the War on Terrorism Be Won?* Watts, 2008.

Ruschmann, Paul. *Point/Counterpoint: The War on Terror*. Chelsea House, 2008.

Woolf, Alex. *Global Issues: Terrorism*. Wayland, 2008.

WEBSITES
www.cia.gov
The website of the Central Intelligence Agency.

www.fbi.gov
The website of the Federal Bureau of Investigation.

www.sis.gov.uk
The website of the Secret Intelligence Service.

www.terrorism.com
The website of the Terrorism Research Center.

www.ict.org.il
The website of the International Institute for Counter-Terrorism.

INDEX

Page numbers in **bold** refer to illustrations.

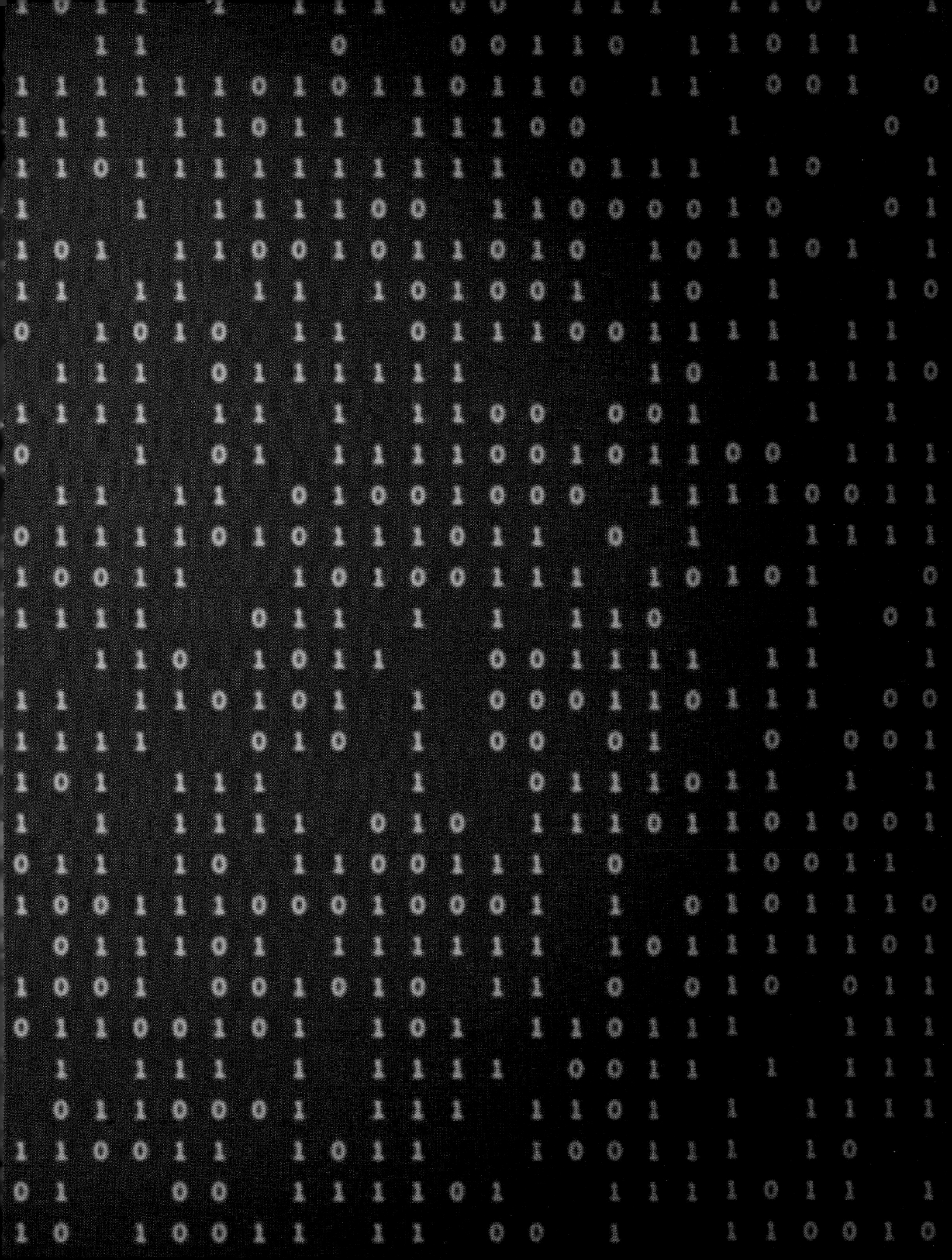